The Cherokee

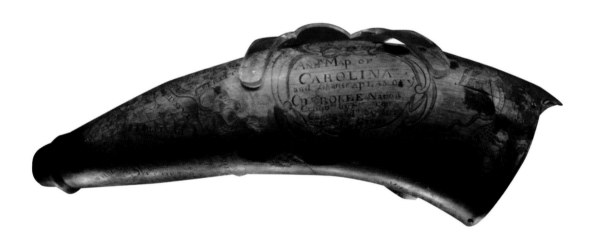

RENNAY CRAATS

PRINCIPAL PHOTOGRAPHY BY MARILYN "ANGEL" WYNN

CHELSEA CLUB HOUSE

An Imprint of Chelsea House Publishers

A Haights Cross Communications Company

Philadelphia

This edition first published in 2004 in the United States of America by Chelsea Clubhouse, a division of Chelsea House Publishers and a subsidiary of Haights Cross Communications.

Chelsea Clubhouse
1974 Sproul Road, Suite 400
Broomall, PA 19008-0914

The Chelsea House world wide web address is www.chelseahouse.com

 Library of Congress Cataloging-in-Publication Data

Craats, Rennay.
  The Cherokee / Rennay Craats.
      v. cm. -- (American Indian art and culture)
Includes bibliographical references and index.
Contents: The people -- Cherokee homes -- Cherokee communities --
Cherokee clothing -- Cherokee food -- Tools and technology -- Cherokee
religion -- Ceremonies and celebrations -- Music and dance -- Language
and storytelling -- Cherokee art -- Special feature -- Studying the
Cherokees' past.
  ISBN 0-7910-7960-0 (Chelsea House) (lib. bdg. : alk. paper)
 1. Cherokee Indians--History--Juvenile literature. 2. Cherokee
Indians--Social life and customs--Juvenile literature. [1. Cherokee
Indians. 2. Indians of North America--Southern States.] I. Title. II.
Series.
  E99.C5C76 2004
  975.004'97557--dc22
                                 2003017517
                    Printed in the United States of America
                    1 2 3 4 5 6 7 8 9 0 07 06 05 04 03

©2004 WEIGL EDUCATIONAL PUBLISHERS LIMITED

Project Coordinator Heather C. Hudak **Copy Editor** Jennifer Nault **Design** Janine Vangool
Layout Terry Paulhus **Photo Researcher** Wendy Cosh **Chelsea Clubhouse Editors** Sally Cheney
and Margaret Brierton **Validator** Lisa Stopp

Cover: Qualla Boundary, NC (Marilyn "Angel" Wynn), Cherokee man (Marilyn "Angel" Wynn), Leg Rattles (Marilyn "Angel" Wynn), Food (Marilyn "Angel" Wynn); Courtesy of Lynne Harlan: page 27; Marilyn "Angel" Wynn: pages 1, 3, 4, 6, 7, 8, 9, 10, 11, 12, 13, 14T, 14B, 15, 16, 17, 18, 19, 20, 21, 22L, 22R, 23, 24T, 24B, 25, 26, 28T, 28B, 29, 30, 31.

Please note
At the time of printing, the Internet addresses appearing in this book were correct. Owing to the dynamic nature the Internet, however, we cannot guarantee that all these addresses will remain correct.

CONTENTS

The People

A thousand years ago, an American Indian group called the Cherokee lived in the southeastern United States. The meaning of the word *Cherokee* is not certain. Some people believe it comes from the Choctaw peoples word *Tsalagi*, which means "people of the land of caves." Others believe it is from the Creek word *Tisolki*, which means "people of a different speech." The Cherokee called themselves *Ani-Yun'wiya*, which means "principal people."

The Cherokee moved north from the areas now known as Mexico and Texas to the Great Lakes region. Their territory covered eight states. They finally settled along the Tennessee River and stayed there for many generations. When European settlers arrived, they began settling along the edges of Cherokee land. The settlers and the Cherokee began to fight over the land.

The Trail of Tears was painted by Robert Lindneux in 1942.

By the early 1800s, the United States government took control of the land. The United States Congress passed the Indian Removal Act in 1830. This act allowed U.S. troops to remove nearly 17,000 Cherokee peoples from their homes in Alabama, Georgia, Tennessee, and North Carolina. Some Cherokee attempted to escape by hiding in the mountains of North Carolina and forming a **band**. The Cherokee were hurt in many ways over the next few years. Between 1838 and 1839, thousands of Cherokee were forced into prison camps. Many more were made to march about 800 to 1,000 miles (1,287 to 1,609 kilometers) to Oklahoma over rough **terrain**. The trip took between 104 and 189 days. About 4,000 Cherokee died from disease, hunger, and the harsh elements they encountered along the way. This journey became known as the "Trail Where They Cried" or the "Trail of Tears." The surviving Cherokee struggled to rebuild their lives.

The Cherokee lifestyle has undergone many changes over time. However, most Cherokee peoples combine their traditional ways with modern ways.

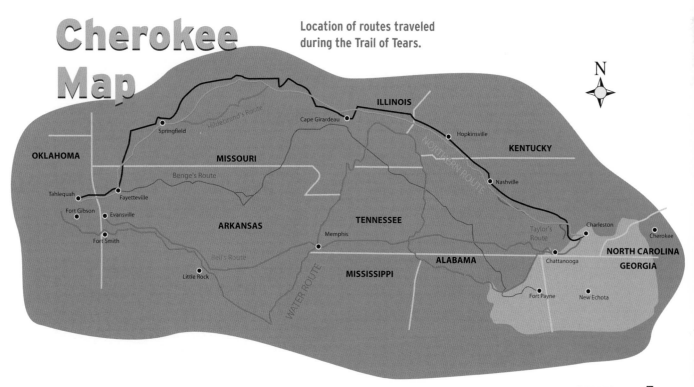

Cherokee Map

Location of routes traveled during the Trail of Tears.

N

Cherokee Homes

Traditionally, Cherokee **clans** lived in villages that were similar to European villages. Their homes were close together in rows that could be miles long. There were usually 30 to 60 homes in a Cherokee village. Each Cherokee village had a town house. Ceremonies, celebrations, and political meetings were held in these public houses. Town houses were circular buildings. They were often built on top of dirt mounds. Benches were built along the inside walls of the building. The walls were made of woven tree branches that were covered with hardened mud. The building's roof was covered with tree bark to provide extra protection from rain and wind.

Traditionally, the Cherokee lived in thatched houses.

DWELLING AND DECORATION

Town houses did not have windows. They only had a small opening for a door. Cherokee town houses were surrounded by a flat yard. Sheds built in the yard offered shade and shelter for villagers who gathered there for community events and special occasions.

Cherokee homes were built around the town house. The households were large because many generations of families lived together. Each household was made up of many buildings. During the summer months, Cherokee peoples lived in large, rectangular houses made from **clapboard**. These houses were usually open buildings that did not have walls. They had grass roofs. Many Cherokee peoples spent most of the summer outside, so they did not need complex homes.

Some Cherokee peoples lived in small, round buildings made from tree branches and mud.

CHEROKEE HOMES

Cherokee Communities

Cherokee society is made up of seven clans. The clans are Bird, Blue, Deer, Longhair, Paint, Wild Potato, and Wolf. Cherokee peoples could not marry a person from their own clan. When two people married, they lived near the wife's family. This is because Cherokee society is **matrilineal**.

Traditional Cherokee society was also **democratic**. Every member of the clan helped make group decisions. Clan leaders could be men or women, and villages often had many leaders. By the early 19th century, the Cherokee began using some of the same governing concepts used by the United States. The Cherokee Nation created a **constitution** in 1827. At the same time, they created three branches of government.

John Ross was the first and only elected chief of the Cherokee Nation.

The Principal Chief establishes laws and policies for the Cherokee Nation. A fifteen-member Tribal Council represents the districts of the nation. This council suggests **legislation** that affects the Cherokee peoples. Representatives on the council work as a team to improve life for the Cherokee. The Cherokee Constitution was revised in 1839 and again in 1976.

Teamwork has always been important to the Cherokee peoples. In the past, men, women, and children all helped tend to daily chores. Children helped to pick berries and collect wood for the fire. Older children watched over younger children, while the adults farmed, hunted, and worked. Often, women tended the fields, and men cleared the fields. Men also fished. Cherokee families continue to work together to meet all the needs of its members.

Modern tribal offices are housed in buildings throughout Cherokee lands.

Cherokee men used a special method to catch fish. First, they **dammed** the stream using logs and debris. Then, they poisoned the water with horse chestnuts that had been ground up. This substance **paralyzed** the fish, causing them to float to the surface of the water. Cherokee fishermen could then grab the fish out of the water using their hands. Then the dam would be removed, and the flow of fresh water would revive the remaining fish.

Cherokee Clothing

In the past, the Cherokee did not wear many clothes. Deerskins were made into short skirts and shirts for both men and women. Children often did not wear any clothing when the weather was warm. During the winter months, deerskin cloaks kept the Cherokee warm. Leather moccasins that laced up to the knees kept the heat in, as well.

European settlers brought many types of clothing to the Cherokee. After the Cherokee were removed from their land, they adopted one unique style of clothing. When they were forced to leave their homes, families had to move away without their belongings and clothing. As a result, women did not have scissors to use for sewing. Instead, pieces of material were carefully torn from fabric and sewn into dresses.

Cherokee capes were traditionally made of turkey feathers. These capes were worn during important ceremonies.

Today, tear dresses are often made from calico printed fabric. They often have diamond, triangular, or circular patterns on them. Some feature the special seven-sided star of the Cherokee.

These were called tear dresses. Tear dresses had three-quarter length sleeves, so they did not get in the way while women worked around the house or in the fields. Tear dresses hung mid-calf, so they did not drag in the dirt. These traditional dresses are still worn.

The ribbon shirt is another traditional piece of Cherokee clothing. It became popular among other American Indian tribes, as well. This men's shirt was made with **calico** material. It had a ribbon design down the front and back. Ribbon shirts had three-quarter length sleeves that were similar to tear dress sleeves.

Today, the Cherokee peoples wear both traditional and modern clothes. Sometimes the Cherokee combine traditional and modern clothing. For example, they may wear blue jeans with traditional belts or jewelry.

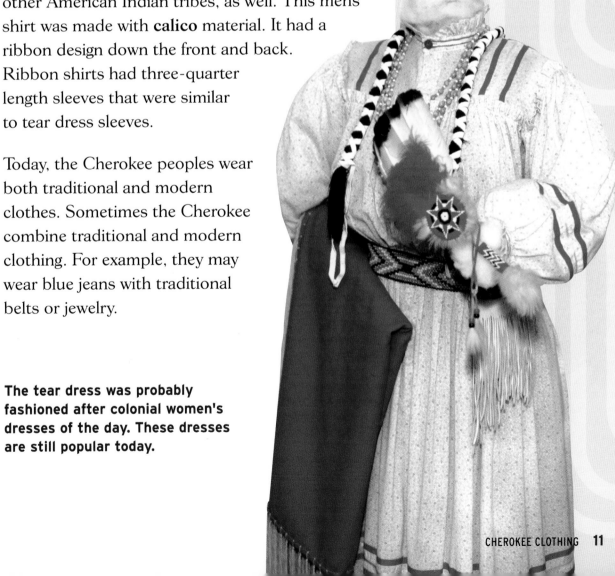

The tear dress was probably fashioned after colonial women's dresses of the day. These dresses are still popular today.

Cherokee Food

Both men and women helped to feed the village. Men hunted wild animals, such as bears, deer, and elk. They also fished. Women planted and tended the crops. **Agriculture** and cooking were chores for Cherokee women. They grew crops of beans, corn, squash, and other vegetables. Corn was a very important part of the Cherokee diet. Corn was used as an ingredient to create many different foods. Sometimes, the Cherokee ate fresh corn. Other times, they dried and ground corn into flour for making bread and other dishes.

The Cherokee ate many foods they could gather by hand. These included squash, nuts, and beans.

Women gathered roots, berries, and nuts. They often dried the fruit from their gardens. They added these foods to meals to create variety. *Kanuchi* is a **delicacy** among the Cherokee. Cooks prepared kanuchi by gathering hickory nuts, letting them dry, and then pounding them to form a paste. The paste was rolled into balls and boiled in water. The balls dissolved in the water and created a liquid as thick as cream. The liquid was then added to **hominy** and served hot as soup. Kanuchi is still prepared today.

Food preparation was not only important for the Cherokee's survival, it was also part of the Cherokee's social lives. Cooking brought women together as they prepared healthy meals for the clan. The food they prepared gave strength and nourishment to adults. It also helped babies and children develop.

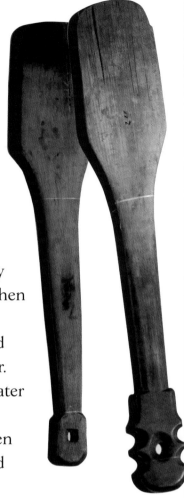

The Cherokee used large wooden spoons to stir pots of hominy.

RECIPE

Bean Bread

Ingredients:

1 cup (0.24 l) cornmeal

1/2 cup (0.12 l) flour

2 tsp. (9.9 ml) baking powder

1 tbsp. (14.8 ml) sugar

2 cups (0.47 l) milk

1/4 cup (59 ml) melted shortening

1 beaten egg

2 tbsp. (29.6 ml) honey

4 cups (0.95 l) drained brown beans

Equipment:

large bowl

baking pan

mixing spoon

1. Place all ingredients, except the beans, in the large bowl.

2. Thoroughly mix the ingredients.

3. Fold in beans.

4. Pour the mixture into a greased, heated pan.

5. Bake at 450° F (232° C) for about 30 minutes, or until brown.

Tools, Weapons, and Defense

The Cherokee peoples were very resourceful. They collected minerals and wood, and used these materials to make tools. Quartz and other minerals were made into tools such as drills and scrapers. **Granite** was ground and polished to make axes and chisels. The Cherokee used wood to make traps for small and large animals. Wood was also used to make valuable tools. The canoe was an important tool the Cherokee used to travel. To make a canoe, the Cherokee cut down a yellow poplar tree, flattened the ends, and removed the branches. Then they covered the log in red clay and set it on fire. Once the clay burned off, they chiseled away the charcoal. This process was repeated many times. It could take up to several months to finish one canoe.

Arrowheads were made from various minerals, but flint was considered the best. This is because flint is very hard and easy to chip.

Some dugout canoes are up to 250 years old.

WAR AND HUNTING

The bow and arrow was an important tool. It was used to hunt large animals, such as deer. To make arrow points, the Cherokee sharpened pieces of bone, chipped flint, or stone. They used the same method to make spearheads, **tomahawks**, axes, and hammers. To make these weapons, the Cherokee used stones to sharpen and grind a groove around the edge of a bone or another stone. The Cherokee used **rawhide** to tie a handle to the groove.

Blowguns were used for both hunting and war. Cherokee hunters used blowguns to blow darts at prey. Darts were often poisoned with snake venom. Young boys learned to use blowguns before they began using a bow and arrow.

The Cherokee did not often begin wars. They fought to **avenge** the deaths of members of their tribe who had been killed by their enemies. The Cherokee believed the souls of the dead could not reach the Cherokee afterlife, called the "darkening land," until those responsible for their deaths were punished. Between 20 and 40 warriors formed a war party. After killing the same number of people as the enemy had killed, the Cherokee **retreated**. Then, the enemy tribe avenged the loss of their killed members with another raid. War was an unending series of raids between nations.

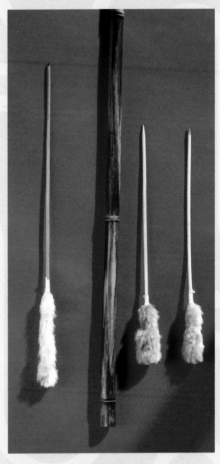

Blowguns are 3 to 9 feet (0.9 to 2.7 meters) long and made of hard wood. The fluff at the end of the dart works to center the dart in the blowgun.

Cherokee Religion

Religion was an important part of Cherokee life. Religion kept balance and harmony. The Cherokee had great respect for the animal world. They farmed and hunted only to survive. The Cherokee performed rituals to apologize to the spirits of the animals they killed. They were so spiritual that material wealth held little importance. The Cherokee took care of both their people and the environment.

Medicine men and women were an important part of the Cherokee religion. These healers treated both physical and spiritual problems. Medicine men and women learned from the teachings of the medicine people from past generations. In fact, every word they spoke and sang during healing ceremonies was said in the Cherokee language. During healing ceremonies, drinking special mixtures or smoking tobacco was used as part of the medicine. This combination of ceremonies and substances was believed to cure the patient. Sometimes, the Cherokee believed witches would interfere with their healing efforts. Witches could trick a medicine person into prescribing the wrong treatment. Medicine people had to be watchful of this sort of evil.

Formulas, songs, and other rites are handwritten in books that are shared by medicine men and women. Sometimes, these words are written in code to protect the information.

In Cherokee religion, humans and animals were closely linked. The Cherokee believed animals had tribes and town houses. They believed animal souls also traveled to the "darkening land." These beliefs explain the respect and importance the Cherokee place in the natural world. Plants and animals, such as the owl, cougar, and cedar tree, are common symbols in the Cherokee religion.

The numbers four and seven are also important. There are four winds, four phases of the Moon, and four directions—East, North, South, and West. The number seven represents the number of Cherokee clans, the number of councilors at festivals, and the number of days between regular **sacrifices**.

Many Cherokee still practice their traditional beliefs, but today, some Cherokee also practice Christian beliefs. Changes have been made to traditional ceremonies, which are being performed less often. Still, many Cherokee peoples are working to preserve their culture.

According to Cherokee religion, beings from an upper world created Earth. The Cherokee religion included many spiritual figures. These figures were an important part of Cherokee life, but they were different from animals and people. Most Cherokee believed they had seen spiritual beings. The Little People were one type of spirit. They were very small people who were invisible unless they wanted to be seen. The Cherokee believed that it was safest to leave Little People alone. If someone saw a Little Person, he or she did not speak of it for 7 years.

The Cherokee Creation story explains how all things on Earth came to be. It is often depicted in Cherokee art.

Ceremonies and Celebrations

The Cherokee held ceremonies and celebrations throughout the year. Many years ago, these ceremonies were performed in every Cherokee village. Today, they are practiced less often. Many Cherokee ceremonies have been changed and updated. Traditionally, there were six main festivals and religious ceremonies commonly held in Cherokee villages. Each ceremony involved **fasting** and feasting, dancing and music, ceremonial costumes, and cleansing rituals that purified the soul.

Many ceremonies were held to maintain or restore balance and harmony within the villages.

Ball game dances were held before the Cherokee participated in ball games. Many ceremonies would take place at these dances.

Many Cherokee ceremonies were important because they called upon the spirits to help make their crops successful. During corn festivals, the Cherokee asked the Sun, the Moon, and the natural world to make the corn harvest plentiful. These festivals took place at the beginning of the harvest, when the dried corn kernels were planted. The largest corn festival occurred when the corn crops ripened. It was called the Green Corn Ceremony. During this ceremony, villagers thoroughly cleaned their homes and town houses. They threw away all broken pottery, torn baskets, and any food left over from the previous year. Old fires were put out, and new ones were lit. All wrongdoings were forgiven.

The New Fire Ceremony was part of the spring festival. Seven people set out to create a new sacred fire. They used the inner bark of seven different types of trees. The bark was taken from the east side of the trees. Once the fire was lit, women took a flame from the fire and used it to relight their home fires. This fire symbolized the spirit of the Creator.

The Green Corn Dance was traditionally held in July, which is the month of the Ripe Corn Moon.

Today, the Cherokee celebrate the Cherokee National Holiday. This day has been celebrated since 1953. The holiday recognizes the 1839 signing of the Cherokee Constitution. It is one of the biggest events in Oklahoma. Each Labor Day weekend, more than 70,000 people from around the world gather to meet new people, visit old friends, and participate in Cherokee activities.

Music and Dance

Cherokee ceremonies were filled with music and dancing. The Cherokee used music and dancing to pray and honor the spirits. Many Cherokee ceremonies featured rattles, drums, and noisemakers.

The Cherokee made instruments from materials they found around the villages. They used gourds, pumpkins, and squashes to make rattles. The pulp of these vegetables was dried out. The seeds that remained inside would rattle when the vegetable was shaken. Musicians added pebbles or corn to make the rattling sound louder. The outside of the rattle was often decorated with paint or feathers.

Noisemakers were another common instrument. Cherokee musicians tied bones, sticks, or nuts together using string. They would shake the strings, causing these items to strike each other and produce sounds.

Today, Cherokee dancing and music are occasionally performed as part of contests or displays of American Indian culture. Singing and dancing helps keep these cultural traditions alive. The Cherokee value art forms such as dancing, music, and songs.

The Grass Dance is an ancient dance that is the basis for many of the other Cherokee men's dances.

CEREMONIAL DANCING

The Stomp Dance performers include a male dance singer leader, assistants, and at least one female Shell Shaker. Women are an important part of this ceremony. The Shell Shaker is the female partner of the dance singer leader. Tortoise shell rattles are attached to the Shell Shaker's legs. The dance singer leader enters the sacred dance site, and the Shell Shaker follows behind him. The Shell Shaker shuffles her feet as she performs her dance. This causes the tortoise shells to make a rattling sound. Today, milk cans are sometimes used as Stomp Dance rattles. The Stomp Dance also includes sermons, feasts, and games.

The Jingle Dress Dance costume includes the jingle dress, matching beadwork, and a fan.

The Booger Dance is another traditional Cherokee dance. This dance tells the story of the balance between the Cherokee and their environment. The dance is meant to protect the Cherokee by lessening the power other tribes and cultures have over them. The Cherokee often wear wooden Booger masks. They paint the masks to look like faces. Some masks have aggressive expressions that are meant to represent enemy warriors.

Language and Storytelling

The Cherokee language was once spoken in every Cherokee home. Today, only about 20,000 people speak the Cherokee language. Fewer than five percent of young people are raised speaking the Cherokee language. However, Cherokee speakers are the seventh-largest group of native language speakers north of Mexico.

By 1821, Sequoyah had completed his table of characters to represent the Cherokee language. This table was approved by Cherokee chiefs, and within a short time thousands of Cherokee learned to read and write.

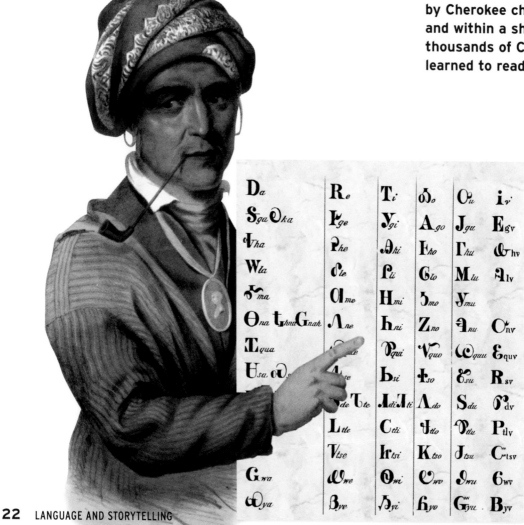

Cherokee is an Iroquoian language, which means it is similar to the language spoken by the Mohawk, Oneida, and Onondaga peoples. The Cherokee language is complicated. For instance, it does not contain the sounds made by the English language letters "b," "p," "f," or "v."

Language has always been an important part of the Cherokee culture. Traditionally, Cherokee storytellers, or myth keepers, could only tell their myths and tales to other Cherokee peoples or American Indians. Before attending the storytelling, a medicine person performed a **scratching ceremony** on invited guests. Then, storytellers would perform the stories. The storytelling lasted throughout the night. After, guests would dip themselves in a body of water seven times, while priests said prayers from the water's bank.

Before 1821, the Cherokee did not have a written language. A Cherokee man named Sequoyah created an alphabet for the Cherokee language. Sequoyah wanted the Cherokee to be able to communicate even if they were far apart from each other. He created a symbol for each sound or syllable in the Cherokee language. This was called the Cherokee syllabary. Using Sequoyah's syllabary, the Cherokee Nation created a written constitution in 1827, and published a newspaper, the *Cherokee Phoenix*, in 1828.

STORIES

Cherokee stories have been passed down through many generations. Storytelling is an art form. Storytellers are actors, singers, dancers, and mimes who tell stories about the Cherokee people and animals. Animals are important in Cherokee stories. Many stories tell of people who could speak with the animals. Some stories tell how the Cherokee could once communicate with animals. According to this belief, the Cherokee lost this ability because their ancestors were greedy and talked too much.

Cherokee storytellers help pass on traditional beliefs.

Cherokee Art

The Cherokee began making arts and crafts out of necessity. When they started, most items they made were objects they used every day, such as baskets to hold corn or masks that were worn during ceremonies. Cherokee arts and crafts are also beautiful pieces of art. There are many different kinds of arts and crafts made by the Cherokee.

Cherokee basketmaking dates back to ancient times. Cane was the most common material used to weave baskets. Baskets were made with two layers of weaving. This made the baskets very strong and useful. To decorate their baskets, Cherokee women made dyes out of such plants as bloodroot, walnut, and butternut. Traditional basketmaking is rarely practiced today. Some Cherokee women still make baskets using commercial materials. These women teach younger generations how to make baskets so they can carry on the tradition.

Cherokee women made pottery using only clay and their hands. They rolled the clay into long ropes and coiled them around to make pots. Another pottery-making method involved pushing one's thumbs into the clay to mold it into a desired shape. Potters used stones to smooth the pot and to carve designs into the piece.

Potters and basketmakers put much care and attention into their work.

Cherokee potters often stamped geometric symbols into the clay. Once the potter finished shaping the piece, it was set aside to dry. Once dry, the pot was baked in hot coals. The type of wood used to fuel the fire determined the color of the pot. The Cherokee often added dried corncobs to the fire to make black smoke. The hardened finished product was unglazed and black. This made the pottery look like cast iron.

Cherokee artists continue to make detailed jewelry using traditional methods. They make jewelry from sterling silver, leather, and beads. Moccasins, belts, sashes, and pouches all show traditional beadwork designs. Cherokee wampum belts are religious and artistic. Wampum belts featured woven words from the Cherokee bible. The Cherokee believe that long ago, a medicine man predicted which warriors would survive an upcoming battle. He split the wampum belt into seven pieces so that each warrior could have a piece. During the battle, the pieces were scattered. The last piece was found about 80 years ago. Wampum belts are decorated with pearls and shell beads. In early times, many beads were made from animal bone or shells.

CORNBEADS

The cornbead necklace is a traditional piece of Cherokee jewelry. It is made of teardrop-shaped beads that are believed to be a gift from the Great Spirit. The Cherokee believe the corn crops watched the Cherokee as they walked along the Trail of Tears. The corn cried and drooped as it watched the Cherokee leave their land. Cherokee women strung the corn's teardrops to create cornbeads, which were worn around the neck. This jewelry is worn as a reminder of this sad time in Cherokee history.

Traditionally, women used smooth stones to make patterns on pottery.

Stickball

Cherokee communities played many games. One game they played was stickball. Stickball built skill and **endurance**. The Cherokee used stickball to train young men for battle and to settle disagreements between tribes. Stickball was sometimes called the "little brother of war."

A stickball game could last for days. The game was played on a large field. Stickball players carried two sticks each with a basket on one end. Players used the basket to catch and throw the ball. They had to hit goals, which were often a tree or rock, with the deerskin ball. Usually, there were about 100 players on each team.

There were no rules to follow in a stickball game. Players did not wear any protective clothing. There were often many injuries, and a player could die during a game of stickball.

For many American Indians, stickball games were used to recreate the story of Creation, in which there was a battle between good and evil. It was even played to honor the dead, cure the sick, and to bring good weather.

A version of this game is played today. We call it lacrosse.

Stickball was played using handmade hickory sticks.

MODERN ARTIST

Jenean Hornbuckle

Jenean Hornbuckle is a Cherokee landscape painter. She was born on the North Carolina Cherokee Reservation known as the Qualla Boundary. Her love of natural scenes comes from her father, who worked as a forester in the mountains of North Carolina. Hornbuckle studied art in high school and later in college. She earned a Bachelor of Fine Arts degree from Western Carolina University.

Jenean Hornbuckle displays her work in murals.

Hornbuckle uses oil paints and canvas. Hornbuckle has studied how European artists' oil painting techniques have deleveloped over several centuries. However, the special look of her paintings comes from traditional Cherokee culture.

Hornbuckle's landscape paintings express the Cherokee's connection to Earth, which many American Indians feel. Through her work, Hornbuckle is helping to **preserve** the beauty of the North Carolina mountains for future generations. She paints on large canvases to show the **majestic** landscape.

Several of Hornbuckle's paintings have been shown at the Museum of the Cherokee Indian in Cherokee, North Carolina. Hornbuckle is also active in the arts community. She helped start the Seven Clans Art Guild. This organization helps Cherokee artists show and sell their work. Hornbuckle travels to other communities to demonstrate her painting techniques at festivals and workshops. She also teaches art classes.

Studying the Cherokee's Past

Archaeologists and anthropologists have learned a great deal about the early Cherokee. They estimate that the Cherokee first appeared between A.D. 1000 and A.D. 1500. This is 500 years before the first Europeans came to North America. Scientists believe that a group called the Pisgah are the Cherokee's ancestors. Archaeologists have discovered villages, tools, and artifacts belonging to the Pisgah. These Pisgah items are very similar to the items made by the Cherokee. From these items, scientists were able to determine that the early Cherokee ate animals, nuts, fruits, and seeds. They also planted crops. The dirt mounds archaeologists found in these villages are clues to the kinds of ceremonial and political practices of these communities.

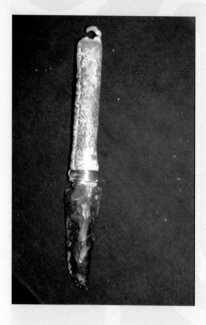

Archaeologists studying the Cherokee peoples have found tools such as knives and pots.

The first written records mentioning the Cherokee appeared in the 1500s. These records did not explain Cherokee culture. The records described the politics of the group and its relationship with its neighbors. By the mid-1600s, more detailed reports about the Cherokee began to emerge. Traders and travelers often wrote about them.

TIME LINE

In the 1700s, records identified five distinct Cherokee groups. These groups lived in Tennessee, Georgia, and North Carolina. Visitors to the area wrote of unrest between the Cherokee, their neighbors, and the European settlers. Conflicts between the Cherokee and several other groups caused the Europeans to forcefully remove the Cherokee from their land. This was the journey known as the Trail of Tears.

Many important Cherokee events have taken place over the years. The following are some important dates in Cherokee history:

Archaeologists have unearthed many Cherokee artifacts.

1821 – Cherokee syllabary is completed

1824 – first Cherokee written law

1827 – Cherokee constitution created

1838 – 1839 – removal of Cherokee peoples along the Trail of Tears

1865 – 1866 – Cherokee peoples negotiate peace with the U.S. government; and new treaty limits tribal land

1889 – unassigned land in Indian Territory opened to European settlers

1934 – Indian Reorganization Act creates land base for tribes and a structure for self-government

1948 – start of the tribal government of the Cherokee Nation

1953 – first Cherokee National Holiday celebrated

1961 – U.S. Claims Commission awards $15 million for Cherokee Outlet Lands

1976 – Cherokee voters pass new constitution outlining tribal government

1987 – Wilma Mankiller becomes first female elected chief

1990 – The Cherokee Nation becomes one of six tribes to take part in a self-determination project to make the nation more independent

Music Makers

Can you imagine life without music? The Cherokee placed a high value on their music. They created instruments and chanted along with the music. Instruments were very important parts of ceremonies. Without drums, rattles, and noisemakers, the Cherokee could not properly honor the spirits.

You can make a Cherokee instrument from materials found around your house. Using several pieces of string, four or five small pencils or dowels, and your imagination, you can create your own Cherokee noisemaker.

STEP 1	Tie a piece of string around each of the pencils. You may want to make them slightly different lengths so they will bounce off each other well.
STEP 2	Collect the string ends together, and tie them in a knot.
STEP 3	Shake the strings. The sound this makes is similar to the sound that would be heard during a Cherokee ceremony.
STEP 4	Use different colored string, and paint the pencils or dowels to decorate your noisemaker.

Further Reading

There are many books that cover Cherokee history and explore the culture as it exists today. A great resource is *If You Lived With the Cherokee* by Anne Kamma, Connie Roop, and Kevin Smith, Scholastic Publishing, 1998.

The Cherokees, People of the Southeast, by Eileen Lucas, The Millbrook Press, 1993, is a wonderful book that explores the traditional and the modern lives of Cherokees in the United States.

Many books examine the Cherokee peoples, past and present. *The Cherokee Indians* by Bill Lund, Bridestone Books, 1997, is a fantastic book for young readers.

Web Sites

To learn the Cherokee syllabary symbols and how to pronounce them, visit
www.nativenashville.com/tutor_syllabary.htm

To learn about the Cherokee Nation, from its government to its history, visit the kid's corner at
www.cherokee.org/Culture/Kids.asp

Learn more about the Trail of Tears and the National Historic Trail at
http://rosecity.net/tears/trail/tearsnht.html

GLOSSARY

agriculture: raising livestock and producing crops

anthropologists: scientists who study human origins, development, customs, and beliefs

archaeologists: scientists who study objects from the past to learn about past civilizations

avenge: to repay with an attack or injury

band: a group of people who were related through marriage

calico: multi-colored, printed cotton fabric

clans: groups of people who are related

clapboard: a long, narrow board that has one thicker edge

constitution: a written document that includes the rules by which a group is to be ruled

dammed: used a barrier to control water flow

delicacy: a special food

democratic: a system of government in which the entire population of a society elects its leaders

endurance: the ability to do something for a long period of time

fasting: going without food, often as part of a religious or political ritual

granite: a very hard gray, pink, and black rock

hominy: dried corn which is boiled

legislation: the process of making laws

majestic: something admired for its beauty

matrilineal: kinship that is traced through the mother's lines

paralyzed: unable to move or feel parts of the body

preserve: to keep safe

rawhide: untanned hide

retreated: withdrew or pulled out of a battle

sacrifices: the act of offering things to gods to show thanks

scratching ceremony: a ceremony in which a medicine person scratches a guest's arms with a comb made from rattlesnake teeth; a healing powder is blown over the red marks left by the comb.

terrain: the surface features of a piece of land

tomahawks: lightweight axes

INDEX